s/rs

A Chicken Followed Me Home!

Questions
and Answers
about a
Familiar Fowl

Robin Page

Beach Lane Books
New York London Toronto Sydney New Delhi

A **chicken** followed me home.

What do I do now?

What will my chicken **eat?**

Chickens in the wild eat seeds, nuts, fruit, insects, and small animals. A domesticated chicken usually eats chicken feed, a mixture of seeds and grains. But if your chicken is free to roam, it will peck at just about anything.

What **kind** of chicken is it?

There are hundreds of breeds of chicken. They vary in size, shape, and color. They may even have a different number of toes.

Naked Neck

Rosecomb Bantam

Modern Game

Plymouth Rock

Buff Cochin

Your chicken looks like a **Rhode Island Red,** a bird first bred for its egg-laying ability. They are good-tempered and hardy birds, which makes them a great choice for the backyard.

Will my chicken fly away?

Most chickens can fly for a short distance—perhaps up to the branches of a tree or over a low fence. But if you feed your chicken and give her a safe place to sleep, she probably won't fly away.

Is my chicken a **hen** or a **rooster?**

tail

comb

beak

cape

wattles

wing

shank

Your chicken is a hen—a female. A hen has many of the same parts as a rooster, but her comb, tail, and wattles are often smaller. Only a hen can lay eggs.

sickles

comb

tail

beak

cape

wattles

wing

shank

A rooster—a male chicken—is usually larger and more colorful than a hen. He is a lookout for his flock and crows a loud warning if he sees danger.

spur

How do I keep my chicken **safe?**

For a chicken, danger can come from any direction. During the day your chicken will stay alert and run to safety if a predator threatens. At night she will need a protected shelter—a coop— to keep out hungry foxes and other animals.

What does a **chicken coop** look like?

Coops come in all shapes and sizes. Most contain nesting boxes filled with wood shavings or straw. Chickens also need a perch—a place to sleep, or roost. The perch may be made from a branch, wooden dowel, or ladder.

Will my chicken lay **eggs?**

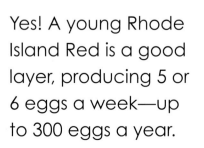

cluck cluck

Yes! A young Rhode Island Red is a good layer, producing 5 or 6 eggs a week—up to 300 eggs a year.

In a year, an average hen lays about 260 eggs. Around the world, chickens lay more than 3½ billion eggs every day.

What if I want **baby** chickens?

Then you'll need to get a rooster! A hen will lay eggs even without the help of a rooster. But those eggs won't hatch. For an egg to become a chick, it must be fertilized. This happens when a hen and a rooster mate.

What happens **next?**

Over a week or two your hen will probably lay 8 to 12 eggs—a clutch. Then she'll take a break from laying and begin to incubate her eggs, sitting on them to keep them warm. This is called going broody. During this time she will rarely leave her nest.

How long does it take an egg . . .

cheep

to become a **chick?**

If a fertilized egg is kept warm and turned regularly, a chick will hatch in about 21 days.

How will the chicks get out of their **eggs?**

A special egg tooth on the chick's beak helps it chip its way out of the egg. This is hard work, and it takes the chick hours to emerge.

Who will take care of the chicks?

For the first few weeks the mother hen keeps her chicks warm and protects them from danger. She leads them to food by clucking. Chicks eat the same food as their mother.

How long before the chicks grow up?

Chicks grow up fast.
When they are just six
weeks old, they will
look a lot like their
parents. A young
female, or pullet, can
lay eggs at around
five months of age. A
young male is called
a cockerel. After
a year the chicks will
be fully grown.

cheep
cheep

cluck
cluck

Now what do I do with all

these **chickens?** Maybe they'll follow . . .

. . . someone else home!

Where did the first chicken come from?

All domesticated chickens are descendants of the **wild red jungle fowl** of Southeast Asia.

When were chickens first domesticated?

Chickens were probably domesticated in India about 8,000 years ago. It's believed that they were originally bred for cockfighting rather than for food. In this cruel sport two roosters are forced to fight each other—sometimes to the death—while bets are placed on the winner.

How fast can a chicken run?

Chickens can run as fast as an average human—about 9 miles (14½ kilometers) per hour.

How many chickens are there?

There are about 19 billion chickens on earth, or almost 3 chickens for every person.

How long do chickens live?

The natural lifespan of a chicken is 5 to 8 years, but a few chickens have lived to be over 20.

What is a group of chickens called?

A group of chickens living together is known as a flock. A small flock can provide both eggs and meat for a family.

What is the largest breed of chicken?

The Jersey Giant is the largest of the chicken breeds. It can weigh as much as 15 pounds (7 kilograms).

And the smallest?

Malaysian Seramas are the tiniest chickens in the world—some weigh no more than 8 ounces (227 grams).

Why do chickens have combs?

All chickens have a comb—a fleshy growth on top of their head. Blood circulating through the comb radiates heat and helps the chicken cool off in hot weather. The rooster's comb is larger and more elaborate than the hen's. A large, bright comb tells a hen that a rooster is healthy and will make a good mate. Combs come in different shapes, colors, and sizes. Here are a few different kinds of combs.

Single

Cushion

Buttercup

Rose

V-Shaped

Pea

More Chicken Questions

What does a fertilized egg look like?

From the outside a fertilized egg looks like any other chicken egg. It contains everything needed to produce a chick.

A newly laid fertilized egg

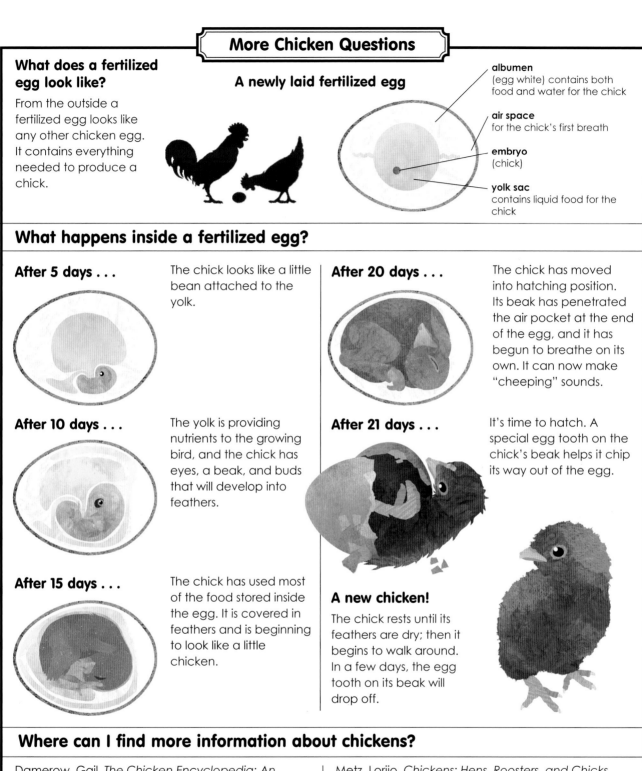

albumen
(egg white) contains both food and water for the chick

air space
for the chick's first breath

embryo
(chick)

yolk sac
contains liquid food for the chick

What happens inside a fertilized egg?

After 5 days . . .

The chick looks like a little bean attached to the yolk.

After 10 days . . .

The yolk is providing nutrients to the growing bird, and the chick has eyes, a beak, and buds that will develop into feathers.

After 15 days . . .

The chick has used most of the food stored inside the egg. It is covered in feathers and is beginning to look like a little chicken.

After 20 days . . .

The chick has moved into hatching position. Its beak has penetrated the air pocket at the end of the egg, and it has begun to breathe on its own. It can now make "cheeping" sounds.

After 21 days . . .

It's time to hatch. A special egg tooth on the chick's beak helps it chip its way out of the egg.

A new chicken!

The chick rests until its feathers are dry; then it begins to walk around. In a few days, the egg tooth on its beak will drop off.

Where can I find more information about chickens?

Damerow, Gail. *The Chicken Encyclopedia: An Illustrated Reference*. North Adams, MA: Storey Publishing, 2012.

Green-Armytage, Stephen. *Extraordinary Chickens*. New York: Abrams, 2003.

Legg, Gerald. *From Egg to Chicken*. New York: Children's Press, 1998.

Metz, Lorijo. *Chickens: Hens, Roosters, and Chicks*. New York: Powerkids Press, 2011.

Percy, Pam. *The Complete Chicken: An Entertaining History of Chickens*. Stillwater, MN: Voyageur Press, 2002.

backyardchickens.com

poultryhub.org/embryo

For Steve, Page, Alec, and Jamie

BEACH LANE BOOKS
An imprint of Simon & Schuster Children's Publishing Division
1230 Avenue of the Americas, New York, New York 10020
Copyright © 2015 by Robin Page
All rights reserved, including the right of reproduction in whole or in part in any form.
BEACH LANE BOOKS is a trademark of Simon & Schuster, Inc.
For information about special discounts for bulk purchases, please contact
Simon & Schuster Special Sales at 1-866-506-1949 or business@simonandschuster.com.
The Simon & Schuster Speakers Bureau can bring authors to your live event. For more
information or to book an event, contact the Simon & Schuster Speakers Bureau at
1-866-248-3049 or visit our website at www.simonspeakers.com.
Book design by Robin Page
The text for this book is set in VAG Rounded and Century Gothic.
The illustrations for this book are digitally rendered in Adobe Photoshop.
Manufactured in China
0315 SCP
First Edition
2 4 6 8 10 9 7 5 3 1
Library of Congress Cataloging-in-Publication Data
Page, Robin, 1957– author.
A chicken followed me home : questions and answers about a familiar fowl /
by Robin Page.—First edition.
p. cm.
Summary: "A nonfiction picture book exploration of chickens and all
the fascinating things about them—how they fly, what they eat, what
the different breeds are, and more"— Provided by publisher.
Audience: 5–10.
Audience: K to grade 3.
Includes bibliographical references.
ISBN 978-1-4814-1028-1 (hardcover : alk. paper)
ISBN 978-1-4814-1029-8 (eBook)
1. Chickens—Juvenile literature. 2. Children's questions and answers. I. Title.
SF487.5.P34 2015
636.5—dc23
2013041955